Steam in and a▮
By Ted G▮

A selection of personal railway photographs.

D**INNAGE**S
—PUBLISHING—

Published In memory of Ted Gamblin 1933 - 2020

Front cover photograph:
Preserved 563, Adam's T3 class 4-4-0 standing outside Eastleigh works. 4th August 1955

Previous page and outside back cover photographs:
653 A12 Adams 0-4-2 outside Eastleigh works 4th August 1955

Cover design using railway colours of the period:
www.clag.org.uk and www.stationcolours.info

Dinnages Publishing
Brighton & Hove, East Sussex
www.DinnagesPublishing.co.uk

Printed in Great Britain.
All original content, text and monocrome photographs: © Ted Gamblin
Additional photographs, map, text and illustrations as credited, or by the publisher.

The right of Ted Gamblin to be identified as the principal Author of this work has been asserted in accordance with the Copyrights, Designs and Patents Act 1988.
All B&W photographs by Ted Gamblin, other images as credited.
Original typesetting draft by Elaine Jenkins.
Book design, layout and additonal compliation by Gordon Dinnage, as the publisher.
Additional contributions by Brian Boddy.
Although every precaution has been taken in the preparation of this book, the publisher and author assume no responsibility for errors or omissions. Neither is any liability assumed for damages resulting from the use of information contained herein.

British Library Cataloguing in Publication Data

A catalogue record for this book is available from the British Library.

ISBN 13: 978-1-8383592-0-1

Contents

Acknowledgements and Bibliography 4

Foreword and about the Author 5

Introduction and about Eastleigh 6

Eastleigh Station 7

Andover Junction to Romsey 9

Romsey 12

Didcot to Eastleigh 13

Eastleigh to Botley 14

Fareham and abbreviations used in this book 16

Netley 19

Eastleigh to Atlantic Park, North Stoneham 20

Stoneham - from early aviation to an important Airport 21

Atlantic Park Hostel Halt, North Stoneham - Southampton Airport 22

Southampton 27

Map of stations 29

Eastleigh Sheds 30

Coaled by crane 42

The Eastleigh Scrap yard 45

Appendices 46

Acknowledgements

The publisher would like to thank the following on behalf of Ted Gamblin for their assistance in bringing these memories to print.

Elaine Jenkins for the original typesetting.
Alan Jenkins for work with text and images.
Andy Nash for scanning the original B&W negatives.
Brian Boddy for his great help with design, layout and additional research.
Joyce Jefford for valuable insights with regard to layout.
John Dinnage in assistance with the Locomotive classes.
Harry Dinnage for cover design and layout.

Bibliography

The following publications were the primary sources used, in which to confirm the author's notes, of his personal research and to further add to the historical accuracy of this book, based on his draft hand writings.

The book of The Stonehams
John Edgar Mann Halsgrove 2002

The Directory of Railway Stations
Butt, R.J.V. Stephens 1995

The Southern Railway 1923-1947: A Chronicle and Record
Savill R. A. Oakwood Press 1950

A Pictorial Record of Southern Locomotives by J.H. Russell
A Foulis-OPC Railway Book.   1991 J. H. Russell & Haynes Publishing Group

Facebook Groups; and other digitised sources:
www.railuk.info
www.semgonline.com
'Eastleigh history and shared memories' for details on locations.
'Disused Stations' for specific station location details.
www.southamptonairport.com/about-us/our-history/
Various other date confirmations were drawn from Wikipedia.

Foreword

The inception for this publication arose through the author, Ted Gamblin having taken many photographs as an avid transport enthusiast in his youth, and later years.

A booklet entitled "Scene Around Littlehampton" published back in 2000 covered many of the road scenes and 'Southdown' Buses captured by this author through his camera lens, which became the first for Ted Gamblin to share his photographs and memories with other enthusiasts and local historians. This book "Steam in and around Eastleigh" follows on from that idea and covers the author's first photographic efforts of Steam in the fifties.

About the Author - Ted Gamblin

Between September 1944 and July 1950, I was a pupil at Chichester High School, travelling each day by train from my home at Littlehampton.

Railways had always attracted my attention, and amongst my earliest memories were seeing engines being turned on the turntable near the small engine shed at Littlehampton, obviously prior to 1938 when the line was electrified.

Soon after starting at Chichester, I learnt that once a week, after classes, there was a meeting of a Railway Club run by a slightly older pupil by the now well-known name of L. G. Marshall and supervised by a Master commonly referred to as 'Gaffer' Reeves who taught German. I joined the Club and consequently learnt that as we left school a little later that day, the journey home could start on the 4.30pm from Chichester as far as Barnham, that train being the daily Plymouth to Brighton through train which had changed engines at Salisbury and was usually hauled by a Drummond 'D15' Class 4-4-0, but occasionally a 'T9' - 'L12' or 'S11'.

From time to time L. G. Marshall would obtain a pass for us to visit a shed; the first time I went on one was to Brighton. Unfortunately, film was hard to come by at that time and it was not until a visit to Eastleigh on the 1st of May 1948 that I was able to take photographs using my Mother's folding Kodak camera which took eight shots - 2¼" x 3¼" on 120 film. It took quite good still shots, but 1/50th of a second was rather slow for moving trains. As soon as I was able, I purchased cameras with higher shutter speeds, but stayed with the 120 film size. The following are a selection of my photographs taken at Eastleigh and in the surrounding area.

Eastleigh lies on the main line running south from Waterloo to Southampton and then west to Bournemouth and Weymouth, lying about ten miles north of Southampton. At Eastleigh there was a large engine shed and also a works where new engines were built and major overhauls carried out.

Relatively few services started or finished at Eastleigh or required a change of engine there. However, Eastleigh shed provided engines for many services from Southampton Terminus, principally boat trains to London, but also for services to Newbury, Alton, Salisbury and Andover.

To the north of Eastleigh Station, a line runs west to Salisbury via Romsey, while to the west of Romsey, a line used to come in from Andover Junction and just to the east of Romsey, a line which still exists, branches off to Southampton. Also north of Eastleigh Station, at Shawford Junction, a line used to run via Winchester Chesil and on to the Western region at Newbury. Another line running eastwards, passed through Alresford and Ropley to Alton. Today, only a preserved section remains, known as the "Watercress Line", running a heritage service between Alresford and Alton since opening in 1977, while at this northern end of the preserved line, Alton still provides a direct connection to the current main line to Waterloo Station.

Just south of the station, but north of the sheds and works, a line branches off eastwards to Fareham via Botley and beyond.

A little further south of Eastleigh Station there used to be a small station called Atlantic Park Hostel Halt, at North Stoneham, which was only operating for about five years. I found it a good spot to photograph both up and down trains, provided you could avoid telegraph poles spoiling the results. Today, that same location has become significant as 'Southampton Airport Parkway', serving Southampton Airport, and the boat trains such as I used to photograph passing by, are now rarely seen.

EASTLEIGH

Opening in 1839 as Bishopstoke, on the third name change, became just Eastleigh in 1923.

1) 30854 "Howard of Effingham" on a down fast Waterloo Bournemouth Train. 14th June 1958

2) 30179 an O2 Adams 0-4-4T seen on station pilot duties four years before its withdrawal from service. 9th April 1955

3) Ex Great Western Railway 5947 "St. Benet's Hall" with a Reading General to Portsmouth train, while a Brighton 'E4' is shunting coaches in the background. 28th July 1953

4) 357, an M7 Drummond, departs southwards from Eastleigh Station. 1st May 1948

5) 30287, the T9 Drummond 4-4-0 'Greyhound', is captured between Andover Town and Clatford with the 6:40 Andover Junction to Eastleigh. 30th May 1956

6) 30283 T9 arriving at Andover Junction with the 7:07 from Romsey. 30th May 1956

7) British Rail Standard 4 76012 is seen near Stockbridge with the 5:24 Andover Junction to Portsmouth. Undated.

8) British Rail Standard 3 82014 seen between Stockbridge and Fullerton. 6th May 1956

9) British Rail 76029 at Andover Town with the 5:42 Eastleigh to Andover Junction.
20th July 1956

10) One of three views of T9 Drummond 'Greyhound' 30707 captured approaching Andover Town with the 8:33 Southampton Terminus to Andover Junction. 22nd May 1956

11) One of two views captured of T9 Drummond 'Greyhound' 30729 leaving Romsey for Portsmouth. 14th May 1955

12) Another T9 Drummond 'Greyhound' 30117 shunting a goods train. 25th May 1956

13) Ex Great Western Railway 2262, a 2251 class 0-6-0 seen arriving at Winchester Chesil with the 1:56 Southampton Terminus to Newbury service. 22nd May 1956

14) A second view of 30707 arriving at Eastleigh with the 10:50 from Didcot. 9th April 1955

Eastleigh to Botley

15) 30745 N15 'Tintagel' leaving Eastleigh for Portsmouth via Fareham. 4th September 1954

16) Battle of Britain class 34065 "Hurricane" at Botley, which had presumably run light from Eastleigh on a test run after repairs. 8th February 1956

17) Ex South East & Chatham Railway 31470, D1 Wainwright near Botley hauling empty carriage stock. 8th February 1956

18) 'U Boat' 31633 at Botley with the 1:48 Reading General to Portsmouth. 8th February 1956

Fareham

A number of lines converged at Fareham, two of which are no more. The branch line to Gosport ceased passenger traffic in June 1953, surviving purely for goods traffic, however two rail enthusiast specials were run on the 25th January 1959 and 20th February 1966. A line running north to Alton, (known as the Meon Valley Line), was uneconomic well before the Beeching Report. From the west, a line comes in, via Botley, from Eastleigh. A short distance along this line is a junction where a line runs to Southampton via Netley. Finally, a line runs east from Fareham to Cosham and Portsmouth.

19) Shortly after leaving Fareham, 'U Boat' 31637 is seen crossing Wallington Viaduct with the midday Exeter to Portsmouth train. 18th March 1956

Left) The Southern Railway crest, the official drawing of the revised version produced in 1947.

Abbreviations used in this book:

SR - Southern Railway
BR - British Railways
GWR - Great Western Railway
LB&SCR - London, Brighton & South Coast Railway
LSWR - London & South Western Railway
SECR - South Eastern & Chatham Railway
NRM - National Railway Museum
NYMR - North Yorkshire Moors Railway

20) Modified Hall 7906 "Fron Hall" at Fareham with the 2:45 Portsmouth to Reading. Undated

21) Battle of Britain class 34066 "Spitfire" arriving with the 1:50 Bournemouth West to Brighton. 23rd March 1957

22) T9 30337 running into Fareham with freight off the Meon Valley line. 5th August 1955

23) Southern Railway N15X class 4-6-0 32331 "Beattie" approaching Fareham with the 1:48 Reading General to Portsmouth. 5th August 1955

24) An M7 Drummond 0-4-4T 30357 running into Netley with a Portsmouth train, in an animated shot of the platform with waiting passengers. 25th July 1953

25) An earlier shot of the T9 Drummond 'Greyhound' 30287 arriving at Netley. The headcode is for a Salisbury to Portsmouth Harbour train. 8th September 1949

26) Southern Railway 30839 just south of Eastleigh Station on a down goods. 28th July 1949

27) Ex Great Western Railway 2240 is also seen south of Eastleigh Station, on a Didcot to Southampton service. 28th July 1949

In 1910 pioneer aviator Edwin Rowland Moon used the meadows belonging to North Stoneham Farm for take-off and landing of his aircraft.   In 1917, during World War l, construction of hangers was undertaken and the site passed to the US Navy.

After the war the site became a transit camp for refugees destined for the United States and by 1921 the hangers had been converted into residential dormitories. At its peak, in 1928, some 20,000 refugees had passed through the hostel. On the 30th October 1929 a wooden halt, aptly named Atlantic Park Hostel Halt, was opened on the London to Southampton railway line close to the site of the Stoneham signal box.
The decline in the number of refugees led to the closure of the hostel in 1931 and whilst the Halt survived for about another five years.

Southampton Corporation purchased the site at Atlantic Park, North Stoneham, in 1932 which then became the Southampton Municipal Airport however still served as an RAF base known originally as RAF Eastleigh before becoming RAF Southampton in 1936. Following the end of hostilities, flights resumed to the Channel Islands in 1945.

In 1959, Southampton (Eastleigh) Airport, as it was then known, was privately purchased by Mr. Somers.   A concrete runway was added in 1963 and passenger numbers quadrupled.   With such a growth in passengers the provision of a railway station was becoming imperative.   With this in mind Mr. Somers approached British Rail and the successful outcome was the opening of Southampton Airport Station on the 1st April 1966.   The station was renamed Southampton Parkway on the 29th May 1994.

Ownership of the airport subsequently passed to BAA who referred to the station as Southampton International Airport, the Limited company name, however records show the name has never changed. Surely an interesting background to a site favoured by Ted Gamblin and, no doubt, other railway photographers to record, for posterity, the variety of steam hauled trains that once regularly ran between Eastleigh and Southampton.

Left) Stephen Hubbuck's 1921 Leyland RAF-type bus HO8312 captured at Amberley on the 19th September 2009 by Brian Boddy. Restored into original livery this Leyland was built for Stoneham Motors of Eastleigh, near Southampton, and was one of six used to transport Russian evacuees from the Atlantic Park Hostel to Southampton until the company went into liquidation.

28) Southern Railway Q Maunsell 30538 heading an up freight. The airport buildings can be seen in the background on the left, with the Stoneham Signal Box to the right. 9th July 1955

29) 30926 "Repton" passing North Stoneham, as the 3:30 Lymington to Waterloo. Stoneham Signal Box can also be seen in this view on the far right in the distance. 9th July 1955

30) N15 King Arthur 4-6-0 30741 "Joyous Gard" heading south with a through train, probably from Oxford. 9th July 1955

31) Lord Nelson class 4-6-0 30851 "Sir Francis Drake" on the 3:30 Waterloo to Bournemouth West and taken from a low point showing track crossovers. 9th July 1955

32) Merchant Navy class 4-6-2 35021 "New Zealand Line" with the up Bournemouth Belle. 9th July 1955

33) Lord Nelson class 4-6-0 30864 "Sir Martin Frobisher" with the 1:23 Southampton Docks to Waterloo. 9th July 1955

34) Third view taken of the T9 Drummond 'Greyhound' 30707 on a down train approaching North Stoneham, and the site of the former Atlantic Park Hostel Halt. 9th July 1955

35) N15 King Arthur class 4-6-0 30764 "Sir Gawain" with empty stock which will probably form an up boat train. 9th July 1955

36) British Rail Standard 4 2-6-0 76007 with a down Bournemouth train. 9th July 1955

37) An M7 Drummond 'Motor Tank' 30377 with a down train. 9th July 1955

There were two stations at Southampton, the principal one being Southampton Central on the main line from Waterloo to Bournemouth and beyond. The second Southampton Terminus for the docks closed in 1966. Boat trains ran to and from Ocean Terminal situated within the docks and adjacent to the ocean liner berths,. Many passengers heading to Waterloo.

38) A second yet earlier view of the Lord Nelson class 30854 'Howard of Effingham', carrying its BR number, however still in Southern lined out Malachite green livery, about to leave with an up express. 8th September 1949

Two examples of platform tickets from Eastleigh Station along with the Southern sign.

39) N15 class 30737 'King Uther' heading west from Southampton Central. 1st August 1955

40) T9 Drummond 4-4-0 30726 is seen reversing the stock into sidings, headcode suggests having just arrived from Fawley. 1st August 1955

41) A 'U Boat' Maunsell 2-6-0 31807 arriving from Romsey with a train to Portsmouth.
1st August 1955

A visual guide of the former lines, stations and connections,
mentioned within this publication. *Not to scale.*

Eastleigh Sheds

Lying to the east of the main line to Southampton and south of the line to Fareham, the Eastleigh sheds covered a considerable area. The actual shed alone covered 15 tracks and was approximately 100 yards long. Both north and south of the shed were large, open yards, the connection to the running line being by a double track running parallel to the main line, with the 'incoming line' curving to the east where there was a modest sized turntable. Two pairs of lines then ran southwards and either side of an office block, beneath a large water storage tank, followed by a coaling stage. Opening in 1903 the Works closed in 1967, read more in a later chapter.

Tracks in the yard south of the shed eventually curved east to an area I never ventured to, but believe they made a 'U turn' to the works where new locos were built and major overhauls carried out. There was also in that area, a triangle where locos which were too long for the turntable, could be turned.

The Eastleigh Works meanwhile opened as a carriage and wagon works by the London and South Western Railway in 1891, and by the end of 1947, the works had built 304 with a further 16 locomotives to follow before steam locomotive building ceased in 1950, gradually changing over to steam and diesel repairs.

42) M7 Drummond 30030, fitted with a snow plough, is standing not far from the turntable. The breakdown train is partly visible in a position where it can be readily mobilised when needed. 19th March 1955

43) Lord Nelson class 4-6-0 30856 "Lord St Vincent" being prepared to work an up boat train. 9th July 1955

44) A later view of the T9 30729 will probably also work a train from Southampton docks. 28th February 1959

45) Lord Nelson class 4-6-0 30862 "Lord Collingwood" standing just south of the turntable, would appear to be in ex-works condition after overhaul. 17th October 1959

46) A second earlier view of 30851 "Sir Francis Drake" was captured outside the office block. 28th July 1953

47) H15 Urie class 4-6-0 30483 between the office block and the coaling chute. Note the coal trucks on the upper line to the right behind the engine. 19th March 1955

48) Ex C18 Q1 Austerity 0-6-0 33018 alongside the coaling plant with piles of clinker in the foreground. 1st May 1948

49) 636 was one of the last two Adams A12's in service with British Railways, still in its Southern lettering, never renumbered, this was withdrawn in October 1948. 1st May 1948

50) T14 Drummond class 4-6-0 in its final form two years prior to withdrawal. 1st May 1948

51) 35001 "Channel Packet" resplendent in ex-works condition. 19th March 1955

52) 35020 "Bibby Line" was modified with lengthened smoke deflectors. 11th March 1956

53) 748 "Vivien" (30748) was converted to oil burning with electric lighting to the cab and to the front and rear head code positions. 1st May 1948

54) 30748 "Vivien" now converted back to coal-firing but retaining electric lighting. 9th April 1955

55) 30434 had spent some time away at Guildford, captured back at Eastleigh just after its withdrawal in February at the Guildford shed, and disposed of in August '55. 19th March 1955

56) An Eastleigh built 30465, finishing service at Nine Elms, is seen back at Eastleigh before withdrawal in January 1956, cut up at Brighton Works in the February. 27th December 1955

57) 34026 Subsequently named "Yes Tor" ran without name plates for an unusually long time. 9th July 1955

58) 34055 "Fighter Pilot" complete with name plates. 9th July 1955

59) 32038 "Portland Bill" recently out-shopped with its BR number but still with "Southern" on the tender. 26th July 1949

60) 34055 "Fighter Pilot" in Bullied style lined Malachite green with no name or emblem on tender. 26th July 1949

61) 30096 one of the original 'B4' tank engines introduced by Adams for use in Southampton Docks whilst 30083 was from a later batch built and modified by Drummond. 16th May 1959

62) C14 Drummond 0-4-0 3741 with Southern Railway, became 30588 under British Railways renumbering, was one of three similar LSWR tank engines still seen in service. 26th July 1949

63) C14 30588 and B4 'Dock Tank' 30082. 9th April 1955

64) 30514 was based at the Feltham sheds, however is seen here on the curve leading to the Eastleigh works with some buildings in the far background. 28th July 1953

The British Railways Station Totem was introduced in 1948 from the influence of The Railway Executive, a modern Art Deco-style curved oval logo was adopted and was proudly displayed at each Regional station across Great Britain, in each of the British Railway region colours.

65) 30496 on the curve from the works to the running shed. 9th July 1955

Coaled by Crane

66) Q1 Austerity 0-6-0 33023. Undated.

67) After withdrawal the locomotive spent some time operating in the USA and Canada. Returning in 1964 to Eastleigh for overhaul. 'Repton' is now owned by the NYMR. Undated.

68) Also preserved, at the Mid-Hants Railway, S15 Urie class 4-6-0 30499. 28th February 1959

69) V class Schools 30939 "Leatherhead" raising steam while on shed. 26th March 1955

70) 30853 "Sir Richard Grenville" 'stopped' for maintenance. 28th February 1959

The Eastleigh Scrap Yard

Although the Locomotive sheds closed as a Train Maintenance Depot in 1967, the site was still used for scrapping engines as late as 2003.

71) 0415 Adams Radial tank 30584 has worked its last train on the branch line to Axminster and is awaiting breaking up. 9th June 1961

72) Adams X6 class 4-4-0 Number 657 on the scrap line. 26th July 1949

Appendix - Locomotives

Photo	Number	Class	Owner	More info	View date	Built	Withdrawn
Cover	563	T3 Adam 4-4-0	LSWR	Restored to LSWR in 1948, to Swanage Railway 2017	1955	1893	1945
Inside & rear	653	A12 Adams 0-4-2	LSWR	Jubilee	1955	1895	1932
1, 38	30854	Lord Nelson Maunsell 4-6-0	SR	Howard of Effingham	1958, 1949	1928	1961
2	30179	O2 Adams 0-4-4T	LSWR		1955	1899	1959
3	5947	Hall 4-6-0	GWR	St. Benet's Hall	1953	1935	1962
4	357	M7 Drummond 0-4-4T	LSWR	Motor Tank	1948	1900	1961
5, 25	30287	T9 Drummond 4-4-0	LSWR	Greyhound	1956, 1949	1900	1961
6	30283	T9 Drummond 4-4-0	LSWR	Greyhound	1956	1899	1957
7	76012	British Rail Standard 4/2 2-6-0	BR	Horwich LYR/LMS/BR	n/a	1953	1966
8	82014	British Rail Standard 3/2 2-6-2T	BR	Swindon GWR/BR	1956	1952	1964
9	76029	British Rail Standard 4/2 2-6-0	BR	Doncaster GNR/LNER/BR	1956	1953	1964
10, 14, 34	30707	T9 Drummond 4-4-0	LSWR	Greyhound	1956 1955 1955	1899	1961
11, 44	30729	T9 Drummond 4-4-0	LSWR	Greyhound	1955, 1959	1900	1961
12	30117	T9 Drummond 4-4-0	LSWR	Greyhound	1956	1899	1961
13	2262	2251 0-6-0	GWR		1956	1930	1959
15	30745	N15 King Arthur Urie 4-6-0	LSWR	Tintagel	1954	1919	1956
16	34065	Battle of Britain Bullied 4-6-2	SR	Hurricane	1956	1947	1965
17	31470	D1 Wainwright 0-4-2T	SECR	Maunsell rebuild 1926	1956	1906	1959
18	31633	U Maunsell 2-6-0	SR	U Boat	1956	1931	1963
19	31637	U Maunsell 2-6-0	SR	U Boat	1956	1931	1963
20	7906	Modified Hall 4-6-0	BR	Fron Hall	n/a	1949	1965
21	34066	Battle of Britain Bullied 4-6-2	SR	Spitfire	1957	1947	1966
22	30337	T9 Drummond 4-4-0	LSWR	Greyhound	1955	1901	1958
23	32331	N15X 4-6-0	SR	Beattie	1955	1936	1957
24	30357	M7 Drummond 0-4-4T	LSWR	Motor Tank	1953	1900	1961
26	30839	S15 Maunsell 4-6-0	SR	Eastleigh LSWR/SR/BR	1949	1936	1965
27	2240	2251 0-6-0	GWR		1949	1944	1962
28	30538	Q Maunsell 0-6-0	SR		1955	1938	1963
29, 67	30926	V Schools 4-4-0	SR	Repton - Preserved	1955, n/a	1934	1962
30	30741	N15 King Arthur Urie 4-6-0	LSWR	Joyous Gard	1955	1919	1956
31, 46	30851	Lord Nelson Maunsell 4-6-0	SR	Sir Frances Drake	1955, 1953	1928	1961
32	35021	Merchant Navy Bullied 4-6-2	SR	New Zealand Line	1955	1948	1965
33	30864	Lord Nelson Maunsell 4-6-0	SR	Sir Martin Frobisher	1955	1929	1962
35	30764	N15 King Arthur Urie 4-6-0	SR	Sir Gawain	1955	1925	1961
36	76007	British Rail Standard 4/2 2-6-0	BR	Horwich LYR/LMS/BR	1955	1953	1967
37	30377	M7 Drummond 0-4-4T	LSWR	Motor Tank	1955	1903	1962

Appendix - Locomotives

Photo	Number	Class	Owner	More info	View date	Built	Withdrawn
39	30737	N15 King Arthur Urie 4-6-0	LSWR	King Uther	1955	1918	1956
40	30726	T9 Drummond 4-4-0	LSWR	Greyhound	1955	1899	1959
41	31807	U Maunsell 2-6-0	SR	U Boat	1955	1928	1964
42	30030	M7 Drummond 0-4-4T	LSWR	Motor Tank	1955	1904	1959
43	30856	Lord Nelson Maunsell 4-6-0	SR	Lord St Vincent	1955	1928	1962
45	30862	Lord Nelson Maunsell 4-6-0	SR	Lord Collingwood	1959	1929	1962
47	30483	H15 Urie 4-6-0	LSWR		1955	1914	1957
48	33018	Q1 Austerity 0-6-0	SR	ex C18 Bullied	1948	1942	1965
49	636	A12 Adams 0-4-2	LSWR	Jubilee	1948	1893	1948
50	444	T14 Drummond 4-6-0	LSWR		1948	1911	1950
51	35001	Merchant Navy Bullied 4-6-2	SR	Channel Packet	1955	1941	1964
52	35020	Merchant Navy Bullied 4-6-2	SR	Bibby Line	1956	1945	1965
53	748	N15 King Arthur Urie 4-6-0	LSWR	Vivien	1948	1922	1957
54	30748	N15 King Arthur Urie 4-6-0	LSWR	Vivien	1955	1922	1957
55	30434	L12 Drummond 4-4-0	LSWR	Bulldogs	1955	1905	1955
56	30465	D15 Drummond 4-4-0	LSWR		1955	1912	1956
57	34026	West Country 4-6-2 Bullied	SR	Yes Tor	1955	1946	1964
58, 60	34055	Battle of Britain Bullied 4-6-2	SR	Fighter Pilot	1949, 1955	1947	1964
59	32038	H1 4-4-2	LB&SCR	Portland Bill	1949	1906	1951
61	30096	B4 Adams 0-4-0T	LSWR	Dock Tank Normandy, by 1972 went to the Bluebell Railway	1959	1893	1963
61	30083	B4 Drummond 0-4-0T	LSWR	Dock Tank ex K14	1959	1908	1959
62	3741	C14 Drummond 0-4-0T	LSWR	Became BR #30587	1949	1906	1957
63	30088	C14 Drummond 0-4-0T	LSWR	ex 3741	1955	1906	1957
63	30582	B4 Drummond 0-4-0T	LSWR	Dock Tank ex K14	1955	1908	1957
64	30514	S15 Urie 4-6-0	LSWR		1953	1921	1963
65	30496	S15 Urie 4-6-0	LSWR		1955	1921	1963
66	33023	Q1 Austerity 0-6-0	SR	ex C23 Bullied	n/a	1942	1964
68	30499	S15 Urie 4-6-0	LSWR	Left Barry scrapyard for the Mid Hants Railway in 1980 for preservation	1959	1920	1964
69	30939	V Schools 4-4-0	SR	Leatherhead	1955	1935	1961
70	30853	Lord Nelson Maunsell 4-6-0	SR	Sir Richard Grenville	1959	1928	1962
71	30584	0415 Adams Radial 4-4-2	LSWR	ex 520	1961	1885	1961
72	657	Adams X6 4-4-0	LSWR		1949	1895	1940

Appendix - Stations

This is a list of the stations captured in photographs within this book with their opening and renaming changes, references and dates.

Atlantic Park Hostel Halt OP 30/10/1929 CL early 1930's
RO/RN Southampton Airport 1/4/1966
RN Southampton Parkway for Southampton (Eastleigh) Airport 29/9/1986
RN Southampton Airport Parkway 29/5/1994

Bishopstoke OP 10/6/1839
RN Bishopstoke Junction 12/1852
RN Eastleigh and Bishopstoke 1/7/1889
RN Eastleigh 9/7/1923

Botley OP 29/11/1841
CL 2/12/1841
RO 7/2/1842

Didcot OP 12/6/1844
RN Didcot Parkway 29/7/1985

Fareham OP 29/11/1841
CL 2/12/1841
RO 7/2/1842

Netley OP 5/3/1866

Romsey OP 1/3/1847

Southampton West OP 1/11/1895
RN Southampton Central 7/7/1935
RN Southampton 10/7/1967
RN Southampton Central 29/5/1994

Winchester Cheesehill OP 4/5/1885 Temporary closure 4/8/1942 to 8/3/1943
RN Winchester Chesil 26/9/1949 Temporary closures 7/3/1960 to 18/6/1960
and 10/9/1960 to 17/6/1961 then finally closed 9/9/1961

OP = Opened, RO = Reopened, RN = renamed, CL = Closed